Reflections of

NARNIA

A FAMILY GUIDE TO DISCOVERING
THE SPIRITUAL TRUTHS

in

C. S. Lewis's classic work

THE LION, THE WITCH AND THE WARDROBE

*A 30-day devotional complete with study guide
for the use of families or small groups*

Eddie Zacapa

Do Good Books
World Wide Web: *www.dogoodbooks.com*

First published by Do Good Books, a division of Do Good Music.

All quotations from The Chronicles of Narnia, © C. S. Lewis Pte. Ltd. All rights reserved.

Scripture quotations noted NIV are taken from the HOLY BIBLE, NEW INTERNATIONAL VERSION. Copyright © 1973, 1978, 1984 by International Bible Society. Used by permission of Zondervan Publishing House.

All scripture quotations noted CEV are from THE CONTEMPORARY ENGLISH VERSION (American Bible Society, 1865 Broadway, New York, NY 10023) and are used by permission.

Scripture quotations noted MSG are from THE MESSAGE by Eugene H. Peterson. Copyright 1993, 1994, 1995, 1996, and 2000. Used by permission of NavPress Publishing Group. All rights reserved.

Scripture quotations noted NLT are from THE HOLY BIBLE, NEW LIVING TRANSLATION. Copyright 1996. Used by permission of Tyndale Publishing House, New York, NY 10020. All rights reserved.

Scripture quotations noted GNB are from GOOD NEWS BIBLE SECOND EDITION, Today's English Version, Copyright © 1992 by American Bible Society. Used by permission. All rights reserved.

Visit us at *www.reflectionsofnarnia.blogspot.com*

Edited by Kathie Lewis
Cover Design by Rachel Zacapa
Layout by Lewis Greer

To Max

My dear father and brother in the Lord who in his dying helped me discover the presence of the living Christ.

ACKNOWLEDGEMENTS

To Rachel, my loving wife, who kept me accountable to not neglect my family during the process of writing this book. Even though it took longer to write than I anticipated, I am grateful to her that I was not lost in the process.

To Andrew and Adam, my little boys, for inspiring me to connect with the child in me. I hope that someday they can read this book and experience its magic.

To my mom for sacrificing so much and for always encouraging me to write and believing in me.

To my brother, Roger, for listening to all of my dreams and silly ideas throughout the years.

To my friend Tony, my Barnabas, who has given me a continual source of encouragement throughout the years.

To Daniel and Troy, who have been two loyal friends who have stuck closer than brothers.

To my friend and mentor, Jeff, who helps keep me on the right path and reminds me of what is really important in life.

To Invia, my counselor, who helps me to see the difference between reality and illusion.

To Kathie for her help with the editing of this book.

To Lewis, whose advice and experience played a big part in the production, design and marketing of this book.

To all the people at Do Good Music for giving me a chance to get all these ideas in front of you, the reader.

To God. For allowing me to put my ideas to words. I could not have written a word here without you. May this work honor you!

TABLE OF CONTENTS

It is the mark of the good fairy-story, of the higher or more complete kind, that however wild its events, however fantastic or terrible the adventures, it can give to the child or man that hears it, when the "turn" comes, a catch of the breath, a beat and lifting of the heart, near to (or indeed accompanied by) tears, as keen as that given by any form of literary art.

- J.R.R. Tolkien[1]

ഏ   x   ഏ

CAST OF CHARACTERS USED IN THIS BOOK

Aslan – The great Lion and the creator of Narnia. He is the King of Narnia and the son of the Emperor-beyond-the-Sea. He represents the Christ-like figure in the story.

Emperor-beyond-the-Sea – Aslan's father, who represents the Father role in the Godhead.

Peter – The oldest of the four Pevensie children who venture into the world of Narnia. He is the High King of Narnia and may be an allusion to St. Peter.

Susan – The second oldest of the children, who is crowned queen of Narnia.

Edmund – The third oldest of the children, who betrays the others as he eats of the delicious Turkish Delight that the White Witch offers him. He may portray Judas in the story. He is forgiven by Aslan and crowned a king of Narnia.

Lucy – The youngest of the Pevensie children. She discovers the wardrobe and tells the other children. She is also crowned queen of Narnia.

The White Witch – Also known as Jadis. We are told that she is half-Jinn and half-giantess. She has managed to take over Narnia by force and has put an evil curse on the land that makes it always winter and never Christmas. She represents the role of Satan in the story.

Mr. Tumnus – A fawn whom Lucy meets on her first visit to Narnia. He is arrested and awaiting trial on account of his kindness to Lucy.

Mr. Beaver – A beaver who can talk and helps the children in their quest to find Aslan.

Mrs. Beaver – Mr. Beaver's wife, who journeys with the children and also assists the children.

Digory Kirk – An elderly professor with whom the children go to live.

Polly – A young girl who travels into the land of Narnia in The Magician's Nephew.

Digory – A young boy who awakens the White Witch in The Magician's Nephew.

Uncle Andrew – Digory's uncle, who has magical rings that allow people to travel to other worlds.

Fledge – The father of all flying horses.

INTRODUCTION

As a child, I recall fondly my school teacher reading the Chronicles of Narnia stories to us. I remember sitting at the edge of my seat, hanging on to every word she read. As she spoke I found myself enchanted, enthralled, and deeply captivated with the magical world of Narnia.

When I heard that the book The Lion, The Witch and The Wardrobe was being made into a movie by Disney, I decided to go back and revisit the magical land of Narnia. Reading The Lion, The Witch and The Wardrobe as an adult, I was once again captivated by the story and found myself delving deeper into the symbolism and hidden treasures that lie behind the pages. The quest resulted in this book before you.

Reflections of Narnia is about taking a journey into the heart of Narnia, focusing primarily on the first book of the series, The Lion, The Witch and The Wardrobe. It is a 30-day devotional/study that makes for a great companion to both the book and the movie by Disney.

I have included some references to The Magician's Nephew because it may help the reader understand The Lion, The Witch and The Wardrobe better. At times the references may be helpful in that they teach us lessons about life that can enable us to understand the bigger picture in more detail.

Reflections of Narnia is intended to give readers a closer look behind the wisdom, symbolism, and hidden meanings of C. S. Lewis' classic story that has captivated millions of readers.

It is important to note that C. S. Lewis did not intend The Chronicles of Narnia to be read as a literal allegory of the Christ story but as a work that most definitely incorporates Christian symbolism and alludes to Christian theology. His work is suppositional—meaning that he wrote in such a way that the reader might see what it might be like if Christ actually did decide to appear in another world, supposing this other world existed, and if he chose to die and resurrect in it as he has done in our world.

In doing this, Lewis reminds us of our story and the greatest love story of all. It is up to us if we choose to become a part of the story today.

We all have journeys that our hearts long to embark on and that for some reason we do not pursue. This book, I believe, will satisfy that hunger and draw you into an adventure that you will never forget—a quest of the soul that you were created to take and have always longed to embark on. A quest marked with difficult challenges, introspection, mystery, miracles, spiritual growth, and a sense of purpose. It is a quest filled with endless possibilities that may even result in entering another realm, one that was hidden.

The Bible talks of this hidden realm and tells us that " ... he [God] has rescued us from the dominion of darkness and brought us into the kingdom of the Son he loves..." (Colossians 1:13, NIV).

Many of us dream of going away to a distant land where our worries and frets fall away, a place where we find ourselves in the midst of an incredible adventure. Like Peter Pan and Neverland, Narnia draws us to a place—despite its being a fantasy world— where the lessons we learn can be brought back to our everyday world and change the way we live forever.

Take in this devotional and journey with Aslan, Peter, Susan, Edmund, and Lucy to the land where you will find hidden truths and pieces of wisdom that can change your life forever.

Enjoy, and prosper.

BEGINNINGS

The eastern sky changed from white to pink and from pink to gold. The Voice rose and rose, till all the air was shaking with it. And just as it swelled to the mightiest and most glorious sound it had yet produced, the sun arose.

   The Magician's Nephew

THE CREATION OF NARNIA

In The Magician's Nephew, we get a beautiful picture explaining the founding of Narnia. We see a lion, Aslan, singing the world into existence. Like an orchestra that gives birth to many sounds and images in our minds, The Voice gives birth to the world of Narnia. We see stars, constellations, and planets appear in the sky as well as grass and trees and animals.

In Genesis we see God speak the heavens and the earth into existence. We are told that "the earth was formless and desolate," and that "the raging ocean that covered everything was engulfed in total darkness, and [that] the spirit of God was moving over the water."

We then read that God's first words were, "Let there be light." With those words, light came into the world and was called "Day." He separates the light from the darkness and calls the darkness "Night."[2] We can only imagine what it must have been like to be present while God created our world and the universe.

It might have been like what we see in the founding of Narnia—or even more spectacular. Like an orchestra can move the depths of our soul with its beautiful sounds, watching God create would have left us completely in awe of his grandeur and creation.

In The Magician's Nephew, Polly, a young girl, experiences an "unspeakable thrill" as she witnesses Aslan's singing and creating life from his thoughts.

This land of Narnia was so fertile that even when an iron bar fell into the ground, it was given life and grew into a lamp-post that gives light.

In John 1:1-3 we are told, "In the beginning was the Word, and the Word was with God, and the Word was God. He was with God in the beginning. Through him all things were made; without him nothing was made that has been made" (NIV).

The Word "logos" to the Greeks was used "not only of the spoken word but also of the unspoken word, the word still in the mind—the reason. When they applied it to the universe, they meant the rational principle that governs all things."[3]

How wonderful it would have been to have had front-row seats to the founding of our world and the universe—To be able to see the mind of God, the reason (Jesus), and the rational principle that governs all things create his most magnificent masterpiece.

Though we were not there when he created the world into existence, we are so fortunate to be able to enjoy the grandeur of God's creation. It is all around us. Whether it is a beautiful sunset, a majestic waterfall, a volcano, or the millions of stars in the sky, God's fingerprints are everywhere. When we look at the next sunset, a baby's smile, or a bird fluttering away, may we remember to give thanks to the Creator who has given us all of this beauty to behold.

> *He is the image of the invisible God, the firstborn over all creation. For by him all things were created: things in heaven and on earth, visible and invisible, whether thrones or powers or rulers or authorities; all things were created by him and for him. He is before all things, and in him all things hold together. - Colossians 1:15-17 (NIV)*

EVIL ENTERS THE LAND

*"Son of Adam," said the Lion. "There
is an evil Witch abroad in my new
land of Narnia. Tell these good
Beasts how she came to here."*
The Magician's Nephew

Just seven hours after the magical land of Narnia is created, we find
that evil has entered the land. It has been brought to Narnia by a
young boy named Digory, whose curiosity got the best of him. In
The Magician's Nephew Digory, who travels to another world by
using magical rings, finds himself before an inscription that reads:

Make your choice, adventurous Stranger,
Strike the bell and bide the danger.
Or wonder, till it drives you mad.
What would have followed if you had.

Curiosity and wonder overtake Digory as he quickly grabs for
the hammer, despite his friend Polly's attempts to convince him
otherwise, and strikes the golden bell with a tap—resulting in the
awakening of the Queen of Charn, better known as the White
Witch of Narnia. From there the Witch seems to follow him
everywhere he goes (even through different worlds) and, of course,
back to Narnia.

We can all identify with some confrontation in our lives that gives
birth to our curiosity and our insatiable desire to want to know
what is on the other side of the curtain. Curiosity is the root of
many people's problems and can take us to places where we do
not wish to go. It also can lead to the discovery and experience of
something remarkably incredible. Using discernment when we
become curious helps us be careful and not be impulsive.

In the Bible we read that Adam and Eve also had a choice put before them that could lead to dire consequences. God had given them one command—to not eat fruit from the tree of the knowledge of good and evil at the center of the garden. And just like when Digory was tempted to strike the golden bell and doubted his friend's good judgment, Eve was tempted by the serpent (Satan) to eat the fruit and doubt God's judgment. As a result of Adam and Eve's curiosity to know the knowledge of good and evil, sin entered the world. The consequence of this action for mankind was separation from God. Yet we find that in God's foreknowledge, he knew this would occur and had a plan to rectify the problem. We are told in the Bible that he had a plan before he created the world to adopt us back into his family by sending his one and only son, Jesus Christ.

We see that Aslan also had this ability to see the future and also had a plan to fix the problem of evil entering Narnia. We see him comfort the beasts of Narnia shortly after they find out that evil has entered their land. He says: "Do not be cast down… Evil will come of that evil, but it is still a long way off, and I will see to it that the worst falls upon myself."

Here we see a beautiful foreshadowing of things to come and of a love that endures the worst for its beloved, a reminder to all of the powerful love of our Creator.

> *Long before he laid down earth's foundations, he had us in mind, had settled on us as the focus of his love, to be made whole and holy by his love. Long, long ago he decided to adopt us into his family through Jesus Christ. (What pleasure he took in planning this!)*
>
> *It's in Christ that we find out who we are and what we are living for. Long before we first heard of Christ and got our hopes up, he had his eye on us, had designs on us for glorious living, part of the overall purpose he is working out in everything and everyone. - Ephesians 1:4-5;11-12 (MSG)*

ALL FOR US

"Creatures, I give you yourselves,"
said the strong, happy voice of Aslan.
"I give to you for ever this land of
Narnia. I give you the woods, the
fruits, the rivers. I give you the stars
and I give you myself."
The Magician's Nephew

Soon after Aslan created Narnia, he gathers his creatures and tells them that everything he has created is for them. He even tells them that he gives them himself. What an incredibly humbling picture! That everything in the world is for those who are his prized creation!

The Bible also tells us that everything that God created is for us and that we were to take care of it all.

God said, "Let us make man in our image, in our likeness, and let them rule over the fish of the sea and the birds of the air, over the livestock, over all the earth, and over all the creatures that move along the ground" (Genesis 1:26, NIV).

The purpose of God's creation is to manifest his glory. Everything he touches turns magnificent and reflects him, the author of life. For this reason we are told that he "saw all that he had made," and that "it was very good" (Genesis 1:31, NIV).

And man, being the last thing created by God, becomes his most special and highly regarded creation. God chooses to not only be incredibly generous in creating everything in the world for man but also decides to make man in his own image. As a result, the glory of God can be fully manifested in man. Like a mirror, man can reflect the Creator's magnificence in his being.

So we see that just as God is sovereign over everything, man is given authority over all the earth and its creatures. Man is to reflect God's authority and sovereignty to the world. John Piper on this subject writes:

> Man is given the exalted status of image-bearer not so he would become arrogant and autonomous (as he tried to do in the Fall), but so he would reflect the glory of his Maker whose image he bears. God's purpose in creation, therefore, was to fill the earth with his own glory.[4]

As a child looks like his father and mother and eventually takes on some of their personal characteristics, so is man supposed to resemble his heavenly father's characteristics (love, grace, patience, self-control, mercy, etc.) when he bears the image of God.

As a result of the Fall, that image or mirror is shattered. Yet God, who knows all things, has a plan in place to rectify this problem and restore the image through his Son, Jesus Christ. This plan consists of Jesus' giving his life. As Aslan says, "I give you myself," our God gives us his Son. And in his Son we find the freedom to live out the plan he intended from the beginning.

> *So then, no more boasting about men! All things are yours, whether Paul or Apollos or Cephas or the world or life or death or the present or the future—all are yours, and you are of Christ, and Christ is of God. - 1 Corinthians 3:21-23 (NIV)*

> *And we, who with unveiled faces all reflect the Lord's glory, are being transformed into his likeness with ever-increasing glory, which comes from the Lord, who is the Spirit. - 2 Corinthians 3:18 (NIV)*

> *This is how we know what love is: Jesus Christ laid down his life for us. And we ought to lay down our lives for our brothers. - 1 John 3:16 (NIV)*

FAULTY ASSUMPTIONS

And the longer and more beautifully
the Lion sang, the harder Uncle
Andrew tried to make himself
believe that he could hear nothing
but roaring. Now the trouble about
trying to make yourself stupider
than you really are is that you very
often succeed. Uncle Andrew did. He
soon did hear nothing but roaring in
Aslan's song.

The Magician's Nephew

In high school I was once mistaken for someone else, and a gang of four or five students started to try to pick a fight with me. One of them even took a couple swings at me. I tried to explain that I was not the person they thought I was but there was no convincing them—they really wanted to believe that I was this person. Eventually, I walked away and as they kept taunting me yelled back some obscene word not worth repeating. Well, shortly after this they all started chasing after me. Fortunately, I was a track athlete and was able to outrun them.

For these students there appeared to be nothing I could say to convince them that I was not the person they thought I was. Sometimes people's perceptions are distorted and, because they do not recognize it, create an illusion.

That is what we see in the case of Uncle Andrew. To him it does not make sense that a lion can sing so he convinces himself that he is only roaring. His distorted perception ends up becoming his reality, and he begins to see the lion and his beasts as dangerous and out to get him. He runs away and faints when they catch up to him and ask him questions—he can only hear animal noises as they speak.

In my work as a counselor, I run across a lot of people who have distorted thoughts that have defined their life and reality for many years. One of my clients, I'll call him Jim, had been arrested for violating a restraining order and physically abusing his ex-girlfriend. Jim shared a memory of his father beating his mother repeatedly with a tree cutter when Jim was just seven years old. His father told Jim his mother had cheated on him. Jim was traumatized and could not sleep for weeks—no one else in the family knew about the beating.

Later, as a young adult, Jim witnessed his sister being beaten by her husband because she was unfaithful. Jim did not defend her but thought to himself, "She deserves it."

Jim then went on to share about his experience with his girlfriend. He said that his girlfriend had been with another man. Because of this, Jim harassed and abused her. The client was able, through this inventory, to see the connection with the first memory. When he was a child, he had accepted (assumed) that it was okay to beat someone if they were unfaithful. This explains why he did not defend his sister and resorted to violence with his partner. By looking back, he was able to find how this belief was given birth and understand himself better. As soon as Jim changed this belief and the belief that he could not live without the victim, he found freedom. He was able to let go of his relationship and move on with his life. This story illustrates the power of distorted thoughts to define our reality.

If we are honest with ourselves, we will discover that we all have distorted thoughts that define our reality. Some of them are there because of our experiences, like Jim's, and others because of things we have been taught by society or our peers. Regardless, the question is, will we examine them and change them?

> *Don't become so well-adjusted to your culture that you fit into it without even thinking. Instead, fix your attention on God. You'll be changed from the inside out. Readily recognize what he wants from you, and*

quickly respond to it. Unlike the culture around you, always dragging you down to its level of immaturity, God brings the best out of you, develops well-formed maturity in you. – Romans 12:2 (MSG)

THE POWER TO TRANSFORM US

"Be winged. Be the father of all
flying horses," roared Aslan in a
voice that shook the ground. "Your
name is Fledge."

The Magician's Nephew

When I was attending San Jose State University, I was invited
to church by a very beautiful young lady I met on an elevator. I
accepted the invitation because I was hoping to get her phone
number. When I went to church, she introduced me to her male
friends and encouraged me to do a Bible study with them. I wanted
to impress her and thought to myself, "It couldn't hurt."

Boy, was I wrong! The first Bible study was on the authority of
scripture and how it was "living and active. Sharper than any
double-edged sword, piercing even to dividing soul and spirit,
joints and marrow" and "judges the thoughts and attitudes of the
heart" (Hebrews 4:12, NIV).

I was convicted and confronted with the reality that I was not
following God in my life, and it hurt. As I continued to study the
Bible, I began to see that my life was not aligned with the things
of God and that I needed to get right with him. I understood that
I was a sinner and in need of forgiveness. I didn't understand why
God would want to call me his child. I thought, "Who am I that I
should have this privilege?" Yet I was relieved at the reality that God
was calling me to himself. After a few months of wrestling with the
truth, I decided to give my life to Christ, and I opened the door
to a new way of living. It was as if I was given wings to soar over
my past obstacles and shortcomings. I was free for the first time in
my life to follow God with all my heart—no reservations. It was a
glorious day!

Fledge, formerly Strawberry, responds to Aslan's question of whether he wants wings in a similar way as I did years ago to God's call on my life. He says, "If you wish, Aslan – if you really mean – I don't know why it should be me – I'm not a very clever horse."

In that instant Aslan roars in a voice that shakes the ground, "Your name is Fledge." And an ordinary horse named Strawberry becomes a winged horse with a new name and the father of all flying horses. In the Bible we read that the Apostle Paul, who formerly was named Saul and a persecutor of Christians, also changes his name when he is converted to Christianity. In choosing a new name, he is disassociating himself with the old man and associating with the new creation that God has made. When we become Christians, we too need to be reminded that we have died to our old lives and have been made new and are now in God's family forever.

Shortly after I committed my life to God someone asked me, "Who are you?"

I answered, "Eddie."

He nodded and said, "Who are you?"

I answered, "Eddie Zacapa."

He nodded and asked me again, "Who are you!?!"

Then it all sunk in. I am no longer Eddie Zacapa. I am a new creation of God. It was the first time I saw myself as a child of God. I answered, "I am a child of God!"

Since that day I can tell of many adventures, trials and blessings that I have lived since I opened the door to Christ. I can tell of the transforming power that worked in me to make me a totally different person—someone who could reflect Christ to others.

When the King of Kings asks you if you would like to be changed forever and given wings, how will you respond?

Therefore, if anyone is in Christ, he is a new creation;

the old has gone, the new has come! - 2 Corinthians 5:17 (NIV)

Even youths grow tired and weary, and young men stumble and fall; but those who hope in the LORD will renew their strength. They will soar on wings like eagles; they will run and not grow weary, they will walk and not be faint. - Isaiah 40:30-32 (NIV)

The horse shied, just as it might have shied in the old, miserable days when it pulled a hansom. Then it roared.... And then, just as the beasts had burst out of the earth, there burst out from the shoulders of Fledge wings that spread and grew, larger than eagles', larger than swans', larger than angels' wings in church windows. The feathers shone chestnut colour and copper colour. He gave a great sweep with them and leapt into the air. - The Magician's Nephew

THE GIFT OF A MIRACLE

*What I give you now will bring joy. It
will not, in your world, give endless
life, but it will heal. Go. Pluck her an
apple from the Tree.*

The Magician's Nephew

Digory, whose curiosity brought evil into the land of Narnia, is
sent on a mission by the great Aslan to bring back an apple that
will serve to plant a tree that will protect the land for hundreds of
years from the evil Witch. As he plucks the apple from the tree at
the center of a private garden, Digory is tempted by the Witch to
eat of it. She tells him he will live forever and will be able to heal
his mother, who is dying, by giving it to her to eat. Digory resists
the temptation and stays true to his mission. He brings the apple to
Aslan.

We can only imagine the struggle and pain of his decision to not
take the apple to his dying mother. He possibly felt like Anakin
in *Star Wars Episode III* when he was helpless to save Pademe and
resorted to the Dark Side to try to prevent her death. Yet Digory, a
child, chooses to do the right thing and obey the command of the
Creator of Narnia.

When he returns to give Aslan the silver apple, we see that Aslan
is pleased. "Well done," says Aslan, with a voice that we are told
"shakes the earth."

Digory is then asked to throw the apple near the river bank where
the ground is soft and fertile so its seed will take root and grow
into a great Tree that will protect the land of Narnia from the evil
Witch. He and the others are told that the Tree will emanate a great
smell that will drive her away. They are told that the smell, "which
is joy and life and health to [them], is death and horror and despair
to her."

We learn that this great Tree is a tree that gives life if its fruit is eaten with the right heart. It may symbolize the Tree of Life in Genesis that imparted life to man. When the fruit of the great Tree is eaten with improper motives, we find that it carries a curse. This is exactly what the tree of the knowledge of good and evil carried when it was eaten by Adam and Eve. Digory is able to resist the temptation that his ancestors were not able to withstand.

Digory, having completed the mission Aslan sent him on, comes to think that all hope of saving his mother is lost. In his first encounter with Aslan we see that Digory is afraid to look up at Aslan's face. He stares at Aslan's feet and claws for most of the time and suddenly, in despair, timidly looks up at the Great Lion's face. He is surprised by what he sees. He finds "great shining tears in the Lion's eyes." Huge, bright tears that reveal that Aslan is as concerned, if not more concerned about Digory's mother's fate. Here we see the love of Aslan that reminds us of the love of Jesus.

Brennan Manning tells a story in the book *Abba's Child* about a little boy who is scared of Jesus, much like Digory was scared of Aslan. The story states that one night a friend of Manning's asked his handicapped son, "Daniel, when you see Jesus looking at you, what do you see in His eyes?"

After a pause, the boy replied, "His eyes are filled with tears, Dad."

"Why, Dan?"

An even longer pause. "Because He is sad."

"And why is He sad?"

Daniel stared at the floor. When at last he looked up, his eyes glistened with tears. "Because I am afraid."[5]

Richard Foster writes, "Today the heart of God is an open wound of love. He aches over our distance and preoccupation. He mourns that we do not draw near to him. He grieves that we have forgotten him. He weeps over our obsession with muchness and manyness. He longs for our presence."[6]

Digory was afraid of Aslan but his fear only kept him from seeing the Lion's heart. Hopefully we will not be afraid to come to God with our cares and requests. He longs to hear them and to be close to us in every way. And in the proper time he will answer our prayers.

When Digory meets with Aslan the second time, he is instructed to go and pluck an apple from the great Tree that was planted. That special apple, when given to his mother restores her health. We find that Digory shortly afterwards buries the core of the special apple in his yard and that it grows into an old tree that is knocked down by great winds years later. We are told that he has the tree cut down and makes a wardrobe out of the special wood.

It is this wardrobe, once discovered, that would lead a young group of children back to the land of Narnia for more adventures to come.

But thanks be to God, who always leads us in triumphal procession in Christ and through us spreads everywhere the fragrance of the knowledge of him. For we are to God the aroma of Christ among those who are being saved and those who are perishing. To the one we are the smell of death; to the other, the fragrance of life... - 2 Corinthians 2:14-16 (NIV)

...On each side of the river stood the tree of life, bearing twelve crops of fruit, yielding its fruit every month. And the leaves of the tree are for the healing of the nations. No longer will there be any curse... - Revelation 22:2-3 (NIV)

UNDERSTANDING OUR HERITAGE

"Good evening, good evening,"
said the Faun. "Excuse me - I don't
want to be inquisitive - but should
I be right in thinking that you are a
Daughter of Eve?"

The Lion, The Witch and The Wardrobe

Lucy, when asked if she is a Daughter of Eve, appears confused and does not understand what the Faun, Tumnus, is saying. She responds by telling him her name. It is interesting to think of how many people would be stumped if they were asked the same question. For some of us the answer to this question is obvious but for others it is still unknown.

That we are sons and daughters of Adam and Eve (the first humans) means that we identify with the Great Story of God. It implies that we have a heritage that is special and divine in nature. If we come to identify with our heritage, we can realize that we were all created in the image of God and that all humanity has been in a fallen state since our ancestors ate of the fruit of the tree of knowledge. We understand who we are and can better understand who God wants us to become. Since Adam and Eve, the original image-bearers of God, the image we were to carry and reflect has been shattered into pieces. Yet when we come to Christ the image is restored, and through time we reflect more and more the image and glory of our Creator.

To forget our heritage is to forget our need for God and the sinful state that we reside in. It is to wander through life as nomads, with no sense of direction and hope.

By understanding our roots, we can also understand why we are the way we are and how our sinful nature works.

Edmund, who is also stumped by the question, "Are you a Son of Adam?" finds himself falling into the Witch's trap. He is given to eat of her delicious Turkish Delight. We are told it is so tasty that it creates a never-ending craving for more—much like the taste of sin.

Edmund, without knowing it, begins to go down the same road that Adam and Eve traveled—the road of temptation and sin. We have all been there. The first thing that happens to us is that we desire something outside God's plan. For Edmund it is power, and for Adam and Eve it was knowledge and power—to be their own God.

Next, we think we need what we desire. We then end up doubting what is true and right. Adam and Eve had all they needed in the Garden of Eden, and they focused on the one thing they did not have. It distracted them and lured them to forget about all they had to be thankful for. Once we are distracted and we doubt and forget the ways of God, it is easier to begin to justify our thoughts and future actions. Convinced that our way is better and justified, we sin.

The end result is shame and guilt and a desire to cover up our transgressions. We want to run and hide and many times blame others for our wrong choices. The consequences of our actions are soon to follow.

The pattern of sin is the same in us as it was in our forefathers. And so is the result the same—spiritual death and separation from God. If we come to understand and learn from Adam and Eve, we can come to understand and appreciate the gift that God offers us—the forgiveness of sins for all who believe and trust in the King of Kings. May we not forget the story of our origins for it, like a boomerang, brings us back to the love of God.

> *And we, who with unveiled faces all reflect the Lord's glory, are being transformed into his likeness with ever-increasing glory, which comes from the Lord, who is the Spirit. - 2 Corinthians 3:18 (NIV)*
>
> *For as in Adam all die, so in Christ all will be made alive. - 1 Corinthians 15:22 (NIV)*

ENTERING ANOTHER WORLD

*"Well," said Susan, "in general,
I'd say the same as Peter, but this
couldn't be true—all this talk about
the wood and the faun."*

The Lion, The Witch and The Wardrobe

SEEING BEYOND OUR LOGIC

Susan and the others doubt that Lucy can be telling the truth about the magical world of Narnia she has discovered. It doesn't make sense to them, and they assume she must be mad or lying. It seems inconceivable to them that there can be anything like what she describes.

Sometimes we also have a hard time believing in what we cannot explain. It is very common for people to frown upon someone who is describing something that appears difficult to understand. Many times our minds will run to the more sensible or logical explanation. "She must be lying or going crazy," we say.

And that is the end of it. We move on and assume we have figured out the mystery. But many times we miss discovering something magical and out of this world.

Hopefully we are as fortunate in those times to have someone like the Professor to open our minds and hearts to the other possibilities, or are opportune enough to stumble into a wardrobe and discover what we kept ourselves from seeing or experiencing.

The Apostle Paul writes in 1 Corinthians 2:6-8 about a spiritual mystery: "We do, however, speak a message of wisdom among the mature, but not the wisdom of this age or of the rulers of this age, who are coming to nothing. No, we speak of God's secret wisdom, a wisdom that has been hidden and that God destined for our glory before time began. None of the rulers of this age understood it…" (NIV).

Here we are told that the message of the Gospel, which Paul is teaching, is not a message clothed in the wisdom of this world but rather in the secret wisdom of God that has been hidden. He also adds, "No eye has seen, no ear has heard, no mind has conceived what God has prepared for those who love him" (1 Corinthians 2:9, NIV).

He goes on to explain that only those who receive the Spirit of God are able to understand this hidden wisdom of God. He also reminds us that God chooses the lowly and despised things of this world to reveal his message and power. Paul writes, "Brothers, think of what you were when you were called. Not many of you were wise by human standards; not many were influential; not many were of noble birth" (1 Corinthians 1:26, NIV).

When we are poor in spirit, God can enter into the depths of who we are and reveal himself to us. It is almost as if he breathes on us his Spirit. It is the humble who have their hearts open to experience the touch of God. The simple ones who know they are not worthy and don't have all the answers are the ones who can comprehend and enter in to the wardrobe of God.

Thomas Jefferson wrote, "State a moral case to a ploughman and a professor. The former will decide it as well, and often better than the latter, because he has not been led astray by artificial rules."[7]

This is what Jesus means when he says we should come to him like a child. He tells his disciples who have been bickering about who is going to be the greatest in heaven, "I tell you the truth, unless you change and become like little children, you will never enter the kingdom of heaven" (Matthew 18:3-4, NIV).

It is no coincidence that Lewis picks children as his main characters in his adventures to Narnia, for they are not so apt to be led astray by artificial rules or logic of this world—though we see glimpses of this in Edmund and some of the others as they struggle to believe Lucy's account of Narnia.

May we not miss out on taking the adventure that God has in store for us and take the detour instead that leads to disappointment, frustration, and a humdrum life. The door is wide open for all of us to enter into God's country. The problem is that many of us never see it, and we miss out on all the blessings God wants to shower on us.

The key to the storehouse of blessings and entering in to God's country is Jesus. When we humbly accept him into our lives and decide to put our faith in him, the magic begins.

> He chose the lowly things of this world and the despised things—and the things that are not—to nullify the things that are, so that no one may boast before him. - 1 Corinthians 1:28 (NIV)

> Still there is a chronic temptation to reduce God to human dimensions, to express Him in manageable ideas. Human reason seeks to understand, to reduce everything to its own terms. But God is God. He is more than a super human being with an intellect keener than ours and a capacity for loving greater than ours. He is Unique, Uncreated, Infinite, Totally Other than we are. He surpasses and transcends all human concepts, considerations, and expectations. He is beyond anything we can intellectualize or imagine. That is why God is a scandal to men and women—because He cannot be comprehended by a finite mind.
> - Brennan Manning [8]

THE GIFT OF DISCOVERY

> *"Quick!" Said Peter, "there's nowhere else," and flung open the wardrobe. All four of them bundled inside it and sat there, panting, in the dark.*
>
> The Lion, The Witch and The Wardrobe

Peter, Edmund, Susan, and Lucy are running away and trying to find a place to hide when they decide to skirt into the Wardrobe as a last alternative. They soon feel cold and are looking at snow-covered trees. These four children were not looking for an adventure into Narnia that day but found themselves in a world that needed their help and had been eagerly awaiting their arrival. It was as if it was orchestrated by providence—as if they were destined to be there. By stepping into the Wardrobe, the four children would discover their purpose and who they were meant to become—the kings and queens of Narnia who would govern in Cair Paravel.

Great stories usually work this way. There is a yearning for something more and then something randomly happens that thrusts our hero into the greatest adventure of his life. Frodo Baggins, Neo, Luke Skywalker, and so many others come to mind. And there is something all these heroes have in common—they all have faith and have said a resounding "yes" to the adventure.

Helen Keller wrote, "No pessimist ever discovered the secret to the stars, or sailed to an unchartered land, or opened a new heaven to the human spirit."[9]

And Steve Prefontaine said, "To give anything less than your best is to sacrifice the gift."[10]

The gift is the discovery. Whether it is a talent or a new world we have discovered, we all have a choice to make—to take the plunge forward or go back to our former ignorance.

Situations have a way of just presenting themselves and when they do, we have the opportunity to discover what we are made of and why we are here. In The Lion, The Witch and The Wardrobe we find that these four children are presented with a surprise and then with a mission. When Lucy finds out that Mr. Tumnus has been captured on her account, the adventure begins.

When we stumble onto the truth of God we must also make some choices. We must decide if we will answer the call and enter into God's country.

St. Augustine talks about how each one of us has the choice of living in one of two cities. He states, "Two societies [cities] have issued from two kinds of love. Worldly society has flowered from a selfish love which dared to despise even God, whereas the communion of saints is rooted in a love of God that is ready to trample on self. In a word, this latter relies on the Lord, whereas the other boasts that it can get along by itself. The city of man seeks the praise of men, whereas the height of glory for the other is to hear God in the witness of conscience."[11]

Which city we choose to enter into is up to us. The choice is ours to make because God has already chosen us and opened the door. He decided to present himself to us and bid us to come to his land. Had he not intermingled with humanity 2000 years ago, we would not have discovered him and been able to embrace him. He presents the Wardrobe for us to enter into. It is not an accident but it is a gift of grace.

> *For it is by grace you have been saved, through faith— and this not from yourselves, it is the gift of God—not by works, so that no one can boast. - Ephesians 2:8-9 (NIV)*

CLOTHED IN MAJESTY

The coats were rather too big for them so that they came down to their heels and looked more like royal robes than coats when they had put them on.

The Lion, The Witch and The Wardrobe

As the children begin to venture out into the forest and become cold, Lucy suggests putting on some coats that are in the Wardrobe. The coats from the Wardrobe look more like royal robes on the children. As the children put them on we are told that the coats came down to their heels.

It is interesting that the coats look like "royal robes," and it is significant that they come from the Wardrobe. We find later on that these four children would rule over Narnia and this appears to be a foreshadowing of what is to come. The reference to royal robes could also be a reminder of something more.

In John 10:9 Jesus refers to himself as the door to eternal life and says, "I am the door. If anyone enters by Me, he will be saved, and will go in and out and find pasture" (NKJV).

Just as the Wardrobe allows the children to enter into another world, Jesus, the Door, allows those who believe entrance to heaven. By walking through the Door we, also, are clothed in Christ and become instantly the children of God, who have a glorious inheritance because we are part of God's family.

Praise be to the God and Father of our Lord Jesus Christ! In his great mercy he has given us new birth into a living hope through the resurrection of Jesus Christ from the dead, and into an inheritance that can never perish, spoil or fade—kept in heaven for

*you, who through faith are shielded by God's power
until the coming of the salvation that is ready to be
revealed in the last time. – 1 Peter 1:3-5 (NIV)*

*Now you're dressed in a new wardrobe. Every item
of your new way of life is custom-made by the
Creator, with his label on it. All the old fashions are
now obsolete. So, chosen by God for this new life
of love, dress in the wardrobe God picked out for
you: compassion, kindness, humility, quiet strength,
discipline. – Colossians 3:10, 12 (MSG)*

FEELING SOMETHING DEEP INSIDE

At the name of Aslan each one of the children felt something jump in its inside.

The Lion, The Witch and The Wardrobe

With just the mention of the name of Aslan, the children feel a strange sensation from within. Most of them felt a sense of hope breathed into them. Peter is described as feeling bold and courageous, Susan as if charmed by a wonderful song, and Lucy with a sense of excitement.

Only Edmund is described as feeling a mysterious horror inside. Something inside of these children is ignited in hearing the name of Aslan. For Peter, Susan and Lucy it is hope, excitement, and courage that spring up whereas for Edmund, it is fear that rises in his heart.

For the children it is as if this name, Aslan, is able to reveal their heart's thoughts and attitudes and either bring a warm message of hope to them or a pang of fear—depending on whether they stand on the side of good or evil.

Many times when we are faced with the truth, our conscience will either feel a peace (because we are right with God) or a strange conviction that may bring fear and discomfort. Edmund felt discomfort and horror.

Aslan is drawing nearer, and with his return will come spring. An old rhyme is recited to the children that tells them of his return:

> *Wrong will be right, when Aslan comes in sight,*
> *At the sound of his roar, sorrows will be no more,*
> *When he bares his teeth, winter meets its death,*
> *And when he shakes his mane, we shall have spring again.*

Soon Edmund's heart will be revealed and the Witch's plans foiled. Edmund can feel this but he chooses to ignore the pang in his heart. The other children find themselves in the midst of an adventure and are given hope and courage to accomplish their purpose and destiny. They align themselves with the right path.

For us, we are told by the ancient scriptures that the Messiah is coming back and on his return he will dwell with us, will wipe every tear from our eyes, and will abolish death and mourning and pain (Revelation 21:3-4). This truth brings us hope and give us the courage to fulfill our part in his great plan. May we listen to the Voice or pang in our heart when we feel a strange sensation within, beckoning us to align ourselves with God's ways and truth.

> *For the word of God is living and active. Sharper than any double-edged sword, it penetrates even to dividing soul and spirit, joints and marrow; it judges the thoughts and attitudes of the heart. Nothing in all creation is hidden from God's sight. Everything is uncovered and laid bare before the eyes of him to whom we must give account. - Hebrews 4:12-13 (NIV)*

> *And we have the word of the prophets made more certain, and you will do well to pay attention to it, as to a light shining in a dark place, until the day dawns and the morning star rises in your hearts. - 2 Peter 1:19 (NIV)*

FOLLOWING THE PATH OF SIN

*And he thought about Turkish Delight
and about being a King ("And I
wonder how Peter will like that?" he
asked himself.) and horrible ideas
came into his head.*

The Lion, The Witch and The Wardrobe

When we are consumed with something, we may begin to doubt the truth and fill our minds with distorted thoughts. This is what we see happen with Edmund. He cannot stop thinking about the delicious Turkish Delight the Witch gave him. He believes he needs to eat it and allows his emotions to control him.

A friend of mine once told me a story of how they capture monkeys in Africa. He told me that they put candy in a cage and leave a small door open where the monkey can put his arm in to grab the candy. When the monkey grabs the candy he has to make a fist, and when he tries to pull his hand out it gets stuck. My friend told me that the monkeys would not let go for hours—the people trying to catch the monkeys would just come up and grab them from behind.

Sometimes we are like these monkeys. All we have to do is let go but we hang on to sin with all our energy. It is amazing how far we will go to not let go. Edmund goes to great lengths to get his Turkish Delight and to try to fulfill his dreams of becoming king. We read that he travels for miles in the snow and is freezing as he works his way toward the Witch's palace. He undergoes darkness, loneliness, coldness, body aches, and bruises.

Often we suffer many consequences as we follow the wrong path and distance ourselves from the truth. It also common, as Edmund did, to blame others for our unfortunate circumstances as well.

Lewis writes, "And every time this happened he thought more and more how he hated Peter—just as if all this had been Peter's fault."

It is incredible how we succumb to the depths of denial when we so desperately do not want to give up something. Edmund demonstrates what can happen to all of us if we allow ourselves to lose our focus and allow temptation's pull to take us down the road to sin.

> Be self-controlled and alert. Your enemy the devil prowls around like a roaring lion looking for someone to devour. Resist him, standing firm in the faith, because you know that your brothers throughout the world are undergoing the same kind of sufferings. - 1 Peter 5:8-9 (NIV)

> For although they knew God, they neither glorified him as God nor gave thanks to him, but their thinking became futile and their foolish hearts were darkened. Although they claimed to be wise, they became fools.... - Romans 1:21-22 (NIV)

ACTS OF PROVIDENCE

But now that the snow had begun
again the scent was cold and even
the footprints were covered up.
The Lion, The Witch and The Wardrobe

As the children are running from the Witch and trying to meet up with Aslan, we see that they get a fortunate break. It begins to snow again, covering the scent of their tracks and their footprints. Is this a mere coincidence or an act of providence?

As we journey through life, there will be times when we venture out in faith and encounter fortunate breaks and blessings along the way. Many times we file them as mere coincidence. But when one after another they continue to happen, it begins to look more like acts of providence.

We also see that the children meet up with Father Christmas, who has gifts for them that they will all later need in the battle against the evil Witch of Narnia. Later on we find out that the snow is melting and slowing the sled of the Witch and her companions. Each of these events helps the cause of the children on their mission.

We are left to imagine how frightening and challenging it must have been for the children to continue on under the circumstances and the toil they would have to suffer. Yet it is as if there was a great plan that was being worked out as they simply lived life and tried to do what was needed to survive and eventually fulfill their mission.

Leigh Nash of Sixpence None the Richer tells of a similar experience where she did not understand what God was doing but later was able to see that he was working out his purpose through her life:

"When I was young my father abused alcohol. And though he was never physically or verbally abusive, he left us all on edge most of the time because we never knew if he would come home sober or drunk. It was frightening and made all our lives feel out of control. But even then, in the midst of her personal pain, my mother tried to keep me and my sister aware of God's reality and what He was doing in our lives.

"We learned valuable lessons about humility and forgiveness, that you could not truly love someone unless you were willing to forgive them. Mom taught us to keep our eyes open for the daily evidence of God's grace. She helped us understand that God was with us even in the hard times, His hand holding ours as we walked the rocky path that stretched before us.

"Looking back on the years our family struggled so desperately, I see that God was working in us toward the eventual goal of drawing us closer together. He was using the events of our lives—the good and the bad, the painful as well as the joyous—to pattern each of us, through our circumstances, into a quilt of bright and beautiful colors. Only from the vantage point of today can I see the beauty and intricate pattern of that quilt. And be amazed by all the grace that stitched it together so wonderfully."[12]

Nash now sees the music that her band produces as a gift from God and as a means to heal their wounds and the hurts of others. She writes of God's masterful work, "I am so much in awe of God's grace. Trusting in His grace, I look forward to tomorrow. And I watch for the new patterns being stitched in my life even now by the Master Quilter."[13]

We do well to remember, like Nash, that Our God is a Master Quilter who stitches a quilt for each of us. Even when we can't see what he is doing, he is at work.

The Pevensie children teach us a very important lesson—to continue with the journey and task at hand. They do not turn back despite all the obstacles they face. We also act wisely when we continue on the journey that God has designated for us and willingly put our stakes down when needed. By doing this we will eventually be able to see the new patterns that the Master Quilter is stitching in our lives. Just as Peter in the Disney film strikes his sword into the ice when pressed by the enemy, we can also be ready to do what is required of a faithful servant of the most Holy King when the situation demands it.

When we act in faith and boldness miracles can happen. Because the children continue forward with their task, they experience the hand of God protecting them. Peter decides to act in faith that something will happen when he strikes his sword into the ice; the mountain at that moment collapses and creates an avalanche that rescues the children from danger. How many times has God rescued his people at the last minute? When we read the Bible, we find that it is a very common occurrence. Walk in faith and know that your Heavenly Father is with you and will never forsake you.

> *And we know that in all things God works for the good of those who love him, who have been called according to his purpose. - Romans 8:28 (NIV)*

> *Keep your lives free from the love of money and be content with what you have, because God has said, "Never will I leave you; never will I forsake you." So we say with confidence, "The Lord is my helper; I will not be afraid. What can man do to me?" - Hebrews 13:5-6 (NIV)*

THE LOOK OF THE LOST

I didn't like to mention it before (he being your brother and all) but the moment I set eyes on that brother of yours I said to myself "Treacherous." He had the look of one who has been with the Witch and eaten her food. You can always tell them if you've lived long in Narnia; something about their eyes.

The Lion, The Witch and The Wardrobe

Edmund was so taken in sin and the ways of the Witch that he had a look about him that gave him away. Sometimes it is obvious to others that we have taken the wrong path, while other times we may be able to hide it. In Edmund's case it was obvious to Mr. Beaver, as the red flags popped up from the moment he saw Edmund.

Many times when we are involved in sin we think we can hide it from everyone. Rarely is this the case. The more we try to hide our foibles and evil ways the more visible our sin usually becomes. Even if we are successful, it is a lot of work. It is amazing how many times people can just see right through us.

I recently attended a wedding where I had an encounter with a woman who had too much alcohol to drink. I caught a glimpse of her eyes as she spoke to me, her speech slurred. Her eyes were glazed, and they looked as if they were carried away and controlled by something. It gave me goose bumps.

People could see that she was heavily intoxicated and acting indecently. Someone apologized for her behavior as she said something offensive to me. This woman was taken by the desire to drink alcohol, seduced and captured by its power. It brought sadness to my heart. I longed to help her find freedom from the path she had chosen.

I am sure that is how Peter felt when he realized that his brother Edmund was lost. "All the same," he says in a rather choking sort of voice, "We still have to go and look for him. He is our brother after all, even if he is rather a little beast. And he is only a kid."

Like Peter, when we see people who have "the look of one who has been with the Witch" in their eyes we should not give up hope but rather see if there is a way we can help them. In my situation with this woman at the wedding, I could have said a prayer for her that she would someday find what she is really looking for and what could fill the void in her life—a relationship with God.

And if we are the ones who have that "look" because we have been living our lives, like Edmund, in the ways of the Witch, let us be honest with ourselves and seek help in the one who can heal all wounds.

> *He himself bore our sins in his body on the tree, so that we might die to sins and live for righteousness; by his wounds you have been healed. For you were like sheep going astray, but now you have returned to the Shepherd and Overseer of your souls. - 1 Peter 2:24-25 (NIV)*

THE BATTLE

"These are your presents," was the
answer, *"and they are tools, not
toys. The time to use them is perhaps
near at hand. Bear them well."*

> The Lion, The Witch and The Wardrobe

THE TOOLS

The Witch has cast a spell on Narnia that it would always be winter and never Christmas. Yet as her spell begins to fade away, we see the emergence of Father Christmas. He brings with his presence much encouragement and hope to the children. There is something about him that any child would identify with. Maybe it is his smile or his great white beard or that bag of gifts he carries with him. But there is definitely something about him that children love.

And to the Pevensie children he brings glad tidings that the Witch's magic is weakening and Aslan is on the move. Father Christmas gives the children presents that will help them engage in the battle that is coming towards them. As Aslan is on the move, the battle between good and evil is drawing nearer. The children will all play an important part in this battle and must be prepared and armed.

Peter is handed a silver shield and a golden sword. Susan is presented with a bow and an ivory horn. And Lucy is given a small dagger and a bottle with a special remedy that can heal wounds. All of these "tools" will assist the children in attaining victory and accomplishing their mission.

We have spiritual tools we can use to engage in the battle before us against good and evil. The Apostle Paul tells us that "our battle is not against flesh and blood but against the rulers, against the authorities, against the powers of this dark world and against the spiritual forces of evil in the heavenly realms" (Ephesians 6:12, NIV).

Sometimes we think our battle is with flesh and blood and we become resentful, angry, frustrated, and overwhelmed with grief over something someone has done or is doing to us. But to see the battle through the lenses of the Apostle Paul is to see there is something more at work in our world. When we realize this, we realize that we cannot engage this force the same way we would if the battle was merely against flesh and blood.

No, we must put on our spiritual armor. Thus, the Apostle Paul tells us, "Use every piece of God's armor to resist the enemy in the time of evil, so that after the battle you will still be standing firm" (Ephesians 6:13, NLT).

Father Christmas has given the children what they will need to stand their ground against evil. We all have experienced days where evil comes and disturbs our peace in God. Evil comes in many forms and shapes and if we are not ready for it, we can be overtaken by it.

As we strive to do our part in the battle against good and evil, we must align ourselves with the truth and carry it in our hearts. This is the first weapon we must make sure we have. If ever, in any battle, we act on misinformation we will suffer serious consequences. For this reason we must make sure we are matched up with the truth of God. In it lies much power, like that of a sword, to slay the lies of the evil one.

Another weapon to carry with us is the breastplate of righteousness. Knowing that we have a right standing with God produces confidence. A breastplate does not protect the soldier's back, but with the proper confidence he will never have to turn his back to the enemy. When the breastplate is on, he we will take the stand against the evil before him, reassured that he will attain the victory. Turning our backs to the enemy leaves us unprotected, just as walking into battle with no confidence leaves us vulnerable before our adversary.

Along with these weapons we must carry in our hearts a deep faith in what we know of the character of God, a secure hope that his providence is at work, and a readiness to announce the truth and free the captives. May we find the courage and enthusiasm the Pevensie children had when they were given the "tools" needed to engage in battle.

> *Stand firm then, with the belt of truth buckled around your waist, with the breastplate of righteousness in*

place, and with your feet fitted with the readiness that comes from the gospel of peace. In addition to all this, take up the shield of faith, with which you can extinguish all the flaming arrows of the evil one. Take the helmet of salvation and the sword of the Spirit, which is the word of God. And pray in the Spirit on all occasions with all kinds of prayers and requests. With this in mind, be alert and always keep on praying for all the saints. - Ephesians 6:14-18 (NIV)

THE WHITE WITCH

> *"Are you my councilor or my slave?"*
> *said the Witch. "Do as you're told.*
> *Tie the hands of the human creature*
> *behind it and keep hold of the end of*
> *the rope. And take your whip."*
> *The Lion, The Witch and The Wardrobe*

The result of following the delicacies of evil is becoming a slave of evil. Edmund finds himself with his hands tied behind his back and a dwarf whipping him and chiding him onward. Here he hits his bottom—he realizes the result of his choice and how far from the truth he has wandered.

This is what the White Witch of Narnia does so well—deceive and trap her prey. She represents Satan in the world of Narnia. She is the mother of all lies and is hungry to steal the joy from the people of Narnia. She, like Satan, has cursed the land with an evil spell and rules over it.

We are told in the scriptures that Satan is the ruler of this world and that his spirit has power over those who are far from God (Ephesians 2:1-2). He is the enemy of God. He is a fallen angel from heaven who chose to rebel against the sovereignty of God. He is the first to betray his ideals for his own selfish notions. He is the lord of selfishness, the master of illusions and the great deceiver. He uses all means possible (people in positions of authority, society, peers, etc.) to deceive us in order to exchange the truth for the lies he wants us to believe.

In Genesis we are told that Satan takes the form of a serpent and convinces Adam and Eve to eat of the tree of the knowledge of good and evil. By accomplishing this, he causes man to sin and a curse to be put on man and on the land. For mankind, the curse resulted in death and separation from God.

In Narnia, the Witch makes it so it is always winter but never Christmas. That it is always winter may be a symbol of death. The exclusion of Christmas symbolizes the devil's wanting to prevent and distort Christ's arrival and mission.

The Witch is always looking for ways to stay in power and prevent Aslan from taking back Narnia and accomplishing his plan. She is using all means possible (including Edmund and her evil creatures) to accomplish her evil means. She will stop at nothing.

According to scripture, our battle is not with human beings but the powers of this dark world. We are instructed to see beyond flesh and blood because there is another force at work, the spiritual forces of evil. And these forces all find their allegiance with Satan, just as all the evil in Narnia finds it allegiance with the White Witch.

Is it a coincidence that the White Witch is incredibly beautiful in stature and appearance? The Bible also tells us that "...Satan himself masquerades as an angel of light" (2 Corinthians 11:14).

Satan and the Witch have much in common. They both hope to thwart the good plans for mankind and to take us away from the truth. As we go through life, we also must beware of Satan's evil ways and enticing delicacies that can so easily trap our souls.

Be self-controlled and alert. Your enemy the devil prowls around like a roaring lion looking for someone to devour. Resist him, standing firm in the faith, because you know that your brothers throughout the world are undergoing the same kind of sufferings. And the God of all grace, who called you to his eternal glory in Christ, after you have suffered a little while, will himself restore you and make you strong, firm and steadfast. - 1 Peter 5:8-10 (NIV)

No one can serve two masters. Either he will hate the one and love the other, or he will be devoted to the one and despise the other. You cannot serve both God and Money. – Matthew 6:24 (NIV)

How you have fallen from heaven, O morning star, son of the dawn! You have been cast down to the earth, you who once laid low the nations! You said in your heart, "I will ascend to heaven; I will raise my throne above the stars of God; I will sit enthroned on the mount of assembly, on the utmost heights of the sacred mountain. I will ascend above the tops of the clouds; I will make myself like the Most High." But you are brought down to the grave, to the depths of the pit. – Isaiah 14:12-15 (NIV)

FORGIVENESS

"Here is your brother," he said,
"and - there is no need to talk to him
about what is past."

The Lion, The Witch and The Wardrobe

As Edmund returns to his brother's and sisters' camp, there are
no accusations or judgments leveled at him. He is forgiven and
received back into the family. We find that he has had a discussion
with Aslan that made quite an impression on him.

In the Gospel of Luke, there is a story of an ungrateful son who
asks his father for his inheritance while he is still alive. After
receiving it, the son runs away to a faraway land and spends the
inheritance on wine and irresponsible living. The story tells us
that he comes to a breaking point when he finds himself sleeping
with the pigs and longing for their food. Coming to his senses,
he decides to return to his father. As he nears his home, his father
spots him from a distance, runs to him, and embraces him with a
hug and a kiss. He doesn't ask any questions and orders his servants
to bring the finest robe and put it on his son. He puts a ring on his
son's finger and sandals on his feet. He also has a calf slaughtered
and throws a feast in celebration of his son's return.

In order to run to his son, the father would have had to lift his robe
and expose his undergarments. For a man of stature and mature
years to do this in that particular culture was unheard of and
shameful. In this situation, we see the father bearing the shame and
humiliation instead of his son. In his running, the father shows the
depth of his love and concern for his son—he cares about nothing
else at this moment.

Note the symbolism involved in the gifts that the father presents
to his son. By giving his son the best robe, he is showing the village
elders and community that his son has his respect. Such a gift was

common for an honored dignitary. It should also be mentioned that during this time, it was not uncommon for a son to be stoned for dishonoring and rejecting his family.

The ring that is given is no ordinary ring. It is the family signet ring. It shows that the son's status in the family has been restored and that he has been given a position of authority once again. In regard to the sandals, slaves would walk barefoot but a son would wear sandals. It was customary to slaughter a fattened calf to celebrate a special occasion or to honor a special guest. And because the calf could feed many people, it was also common to invite the whole community to the celebration.

This story shows a father's love and focus on how special and worthy we are of being his children—no matter what we have done or how far we have wandered.

Likewise, Aslan sends a party to rescue Edmund and forgives him for his betrayal to his siblings and the cause. He presents Edmund to Peter, Lucy, and Susan as one who has been forgiven and restored—the past forgotten. His rightful place as one of the kings of Narnia is not lost, but still intact.

We also see a father's love in Aslan as he willingly sacrifices his life for Edmund's. As we can imagine the father in the parable of the prodigal son running toward his son with his robe waving in the wind, we see Aslan not concerned with his appearance as he is shaved of his beautiful fur to restore and save Edmund. We see a magnificent picture of a love that is willing to sacrifice all to redeem one who was lost.

> *For God so loved the world that he gave his one and only Son, that whoever believes in him shall not perish but have eternal life. - John 3:16 (NIV)*
>
> *So he got up and went to his father. But while he was still a long way off, his father saw him and was filled with compassion for him; he ran to his son, threw his arms around him and kissed him. - Luke 15:20 (NIV)*

THE CURSE

> *"He [Aslan] knows the Deep Magic better than that. He knows that unless I have blood as the Law says, all Narnia will be overturned and perish in fire and water."*
>
> The Lion, The Witch and The Wardrobe

As the Witch speaks with Aslan in a special meeting, she points out that Edmund has broken the law. She reminds everyone what is engraved on the Stone Table (and the scepter that belongs to the Emperor-beyond-the-Sea). She says that she has a right to every traitor in Narnia, and that she can kill those who commit treachery. The Witch was the Emperor's hangman.

It appears that from this hangman role she came to imagine herself a queen. Before explaining the curse, it may be helpful for us to understand some background on why she believes she believes she should be queen of Narnia.

The Witch gives two reasons why she should have rightful ownership of this office, both of which are false claims. First, she states that she is human when she is not. Though she appears human, we are told that she is a descendent of Adam's first wife, Lilith (one of the Djinn), and on the other side half-giant. The progeny of these two races (the Djinn and the giants) inhabited Charn, the world that the Witch came from and destroyed.

This concept of Adam having another wife arose in the Middle Ages from The Alphabet of Ben Sira, an anonymous work of fiction. It was believed that Adam's first wife ran away after countless feuding. According to the story, three angels were sent to bring her back but she refused and vowed to prey eternally on Adam and Eve's children.

The second reason the Witch gives for her title of queen is that she was the Emperor's hangman and served him under his and Aslan's blessing. She apparently believed that she could assume the throne because of this.

We can see clearly that she is full of treachery, but she still has enough influence, it appears, to ask for Edmund's life. Of course her true intention here is to spoil Aslan's plans to position the four children in their rightful thrones to rule over Narnia. If there are only three children left to rule, the prophecy will not be fulfilled and the children will not be able to assume their predestined roles.

Aslan recognizes that what is engraved in the Stone Table (and the Deep Magic) must be respected and offers his life in exchange for Edmund's. Scripture instructs us that Jesus also offers his life voluntarily as a ransom for our sins. It tells us that we were dead in our sins and doomed by the law to be eternally separated from God.

We are told in Colossians 2:13-15 (CEV), "You were dead, because you were sinful and were not God's people. But God let Christ make you alive, when he forgave all our sins. God wiped out the charges that were against us for disobeying the Law of Moses. He took them away and nailed them to the cross. There Christ defeated all the powers and forces."

The Stone Table represents the Law of Moses and its curse on us all. Because no one can keep the whole law we are all held accountable to the penalty, which is eternal separation from God. But God, in Christ, pays the price of our sins and redeems those who put their faith in Christ. Through his resurrection we can all be free to live eternally and experience his wonderful and all encompassing love.

> *Christ redeemed us from the curse of the law by becoming a curse for us, for it is written: "Cursed is everyone who is hung on a tree." - Galatians 3:13 (NIV)*

> *This is how we know what love is: Jesus Christ laid down his life for us. And we ought to lay down our lives for our brothers. - 1 John 3:16 (NIV)*

THE REVERENT SUBMISSION

He looked somehow different from
the Aslan they knew. His tail and his
head hung low and he walked slowly
as if he were very, very tired.

The Lion, The Witch and The Wardrobe

As Aslan starts to make his way to the Stone Table to sacrifice himself, the children notice that he is acting differently than normal and that he seems to be carrying a heavy burden in his heart. He is walking slowly and drooping, dreading what is to come.

This is reminiscent of what Jesus must have felt like the night he was arrested and betrayed. Jesus asked for prayer from his disciples that night and we are told that he was deeply distressed and sorrowful "to the point of death" (Matthew 26:36-38, NIV).

Jesus, knowing that he was going to sacrifice himself for the sins of humanity, asks God the Father "if it is possible, may this cup be taken from me. Yet not as I will, but as you will" (Matthew 26:39, NIV).

Here we catch a glimpse of the internal struggle of Jesus and how difficult it must have been for him to lay down his life. In the Gospel of Luke we are told that Jesus' sweat was "like drops of blood falling to the ground" (Luke 22:44, NIV).

And scripture adds that, "During the days of Jesus' life on earth, he offered up prayers and petitions with loud cries and tears to the one who could save him from death, and he was heard because of his reverent submission. Although he was a son, he learned obedience from what he suffered and, once made perfect, he became the source of eternal salvation for all who obey him" (Hebrews 5:7-9, NIV).

Through Jesus' death—"the reverent submission"—he was made perfect (his purpose complete) and thus became the source of eternal life. As Aslan heads toward the Stone Table we should all be reminded of the great resolve that Jesus demonstrated on his journey to the cross.

> *He took Peter and the two sons of Zebedee along with him, and he began to be sorrowful and troubled. Then he said to them, "My soul is overwhelmed with sorrow to the point of death. Stay here and keep watch with me." Going a little farther, he fell with his face to the ground and prayed, "My Father, if it is possible, may this cup be taken from me. Yet not as I will, but as you will." - Matthew 26:37-39 (NIV)*

THE SACRIFICE

...had the Lion chosen, one of those paws could have been the death of them all.

The Lion, The Witch and The Wardrobe

On his own accord, Aslan lays down his life. At any moment he could have unleashed his power and those mighty paws and ended the torture that was to come. Yet we find him resolved and committed to fulfilling the sacrifice that must be accomplished.

The Gospel of Matthew records that after Peter drew his sword and cut off a soldier's ear, Jesus told him: "Do you think I cannot call on my Father, and he will at once put at my disposal more than twelve legions of angels? But how then would the scriptures be fulfilled that say it must happen in this way?" (Matthew 26:53-54, NIV).

As Aslan is bound, we see a series of things occur that break our heart. We see his enemies jeering and mocking him in a revolting way. We see him shaved of his beautiful mane and ridiculed. He is kicked, hit, and spit on in unison.

To add more insult to injury, we hear the evil Witch gloating and telling him that when he is dead she will violate their pact and kill Edmund as well, and that Narnia will be hers to rule forever. In the Disney film she sarcastically remarks, "So much for love" and ends her venomous words with, "In that knowledge, despair and die."

At that moment of Aslan's death we all want to look away. And that is just what we find the two Daughters of Eve doing. Though speculative, this may have also been how God the Father must have felt and may have reacted to his Son, Jesus, dying on the cross. How horrid would it have been to see your only begotten son die in such a painful way?

We are told in Isaiah how sin affects our relationship with God. It reads: "Surely the arm of the Lord is not too short to save, nor his ear too dull to hear. But your iniquities have separated you from your God; your sins have hidden his face from you, so that he will not hear" (Isaiah 59:1-2, NIV).

It makes sense, therefore, that since Christ took on our sin that he would suffer the same consequence—separation from God. This separation must have been the worst thing he had ever endured, even death. He had never been separated from the Father and this is what he must have dreaded most.

Imagine God the Father turning away because he could not bear to watch the sins of the world fall on his beloved Son. And then to hear Jesus cry out, "My God, my God, why have you forsaken me?" (Mark 15:34, NIV).

The Father allows all of this to happen so that the sacrifice can be made complete and the price of sin paid—he loves us that much. May we never forget the cost of the sacrifice and the depth, the length, the height and the width of his great love for us.

> *...And I pray that you, being rooted and established in love, may have power, together with all the saints, to grasp how wide and long and high and deep is the love of Christ, and to know this love that surpasses knowledge—that you may be filled to the measure of all the fullness of God. - Ephesians 3:17-19 (NIV)*

> *For I am convinced that neither death nor life, neither angels nor demons, neither the present nor the future, nor any powers, neither height nor depth, nor anything else in all creation, will be able to separate us from the love of God that is in Christ Jesus our Lord. - Romans 8:38-39 (NIV)*

THE VICTORY

At that moment they heard from behind them a loud noise—a great cracking, deafening noise as if a giant had broken a giant's plate.

The Lion, The Witch and The Wardrobe

THE STONE TABLE CRACKS

As Susan and Lucy are walking away they hear a "cracking, deafening noise," and they are frightened to turn around. They are concerned that the Witch and her agents are doing something worse to Aslan and, when they turn, they find the Stone Table bare and broken in two.

The breaking of the Stone Table, which symbolizes the Law of Moses and the Old Covenant, is similar to the way in which the curtain guarding the holy sanctuary of the temple "tore in two from top to bottom" (Matthew 27:51, NIV). The curtain had reminded everyone of the separation between God and man because of sin.

According to the Old Covenant, only the high priest could enter into this holiest place once a year. After Jesus' death on the cross, the magnificent and thick curtain tore in two; symbolizing that anyone could now have access to God through the blood of Jesus.

Prior to Christ's death on the cross, the high priest would sacrifice an animal on the altar of the holy sanctuary. This was an annual tradition, representing or symbolizing access made available to God through an atoning sacrifice. Christ's providing the atoning sacrifice for all mankind meant there was no more need for animal sacrifices or a curtain to separate man from God. Anyone who believed in Christ could enter into the holiest of holies, the throne room of God.

We are no longer bound by the Old Covenant Law but freed by the blood of Christ to enter into a New Covenant brought in by Jesus. The stronghold of Satan's power that held death and Hades has been broken. The Lamb of God now holds the keys to eternal life and offers them to all who believe.

In Narnia, the Witch's power over the land was broken and the long 100 year winter was over. A new reign would soon be implemented in Narnia with the Pevensie children sitting on the four thrones at

Cair Paravel. The Stone Table breaking symbolizes that the magic before the dawn of time has no more power over Narnia. The Stone Table was no longer needed and of use in the new era to come; an era where grace, forgiveness, and restoration would reign.

> *And so, dear brothers and sisters, we can boldly enter heaven's Most Holy Place because of the blood of Jesus. This is the new, life-giving way that Christ has opened up for us through the sacred curtain, by means of his death for us. And since we have a great High Priest who rules over God's people, let us go right into the presence of God, with true hearts fully trusting him. For our evil consciences have been sprinkled with Christ's blood to make us clean, and our bodies have been washed with pure water. Without wavering, let us hold tightly to the hope we say we have, for God can be trusted to keep his promise. - Hebrews 10:19-23 (NLT)*

THE WITNESSES

"Who's done it?" cried Susan. "What
does it mean? Is it magic?"

The Lion, The Witch and The Wardrobe

Susan and Lucy, who have spent the whole night with Aslan and
witnessed his death, are confused and startled seeing the Stone
Table bare. The two girls think that the body of Aslan has been
stolen. Lucy begins to sob and Susan to ask questions.

Suddenly from behind them they hear the great familiar voice of
Aslan state with a resounding, "Yes!… It is more magic."

What an incredible moment that must have been. Once convinced
that he is not a ghost, the girls "flung themselves upon him and
covered him with kisses."

According to the Gospel of Matthew, Mary Magdalene and Mary
the mother of James arrive at Jesus' tomb to find it empty (Matthew
28:1-6). In John 20:14-17 we read that Mary Magdalene thinks
Jesus' body has been stolen and that she weeps in front of Jesus
(not knowing it is him and thinking he is a gardener). Jesus shouts,
"Mary!" and she is suddenly able to recognize him.

We are also told that when Jesus appeared to both Mary Magdalene
and the other Mary that they "ran to him, held his feet and
worshipped him" (Matthew 28:9, NLT).

It is never too late to realize what Jesus has done for us and to get
on our knees and adore him. May we take time out of our busy
schedules to worship the King of Kings who conquered death and
who is seated at the right hand of God.

Then I looked and heard the voice of many angels,
numbering thousands upon thousands, and ten
thousand times ten thousand. They encircled the

throne and the living creatures and the elders. In a loud voice they sang: "Worthy is the Lamb, who was slain, to receive power and wealth and wisdom and strength and honor and glory and praise!"

Then I heard every creature in heaven and on earth and under the earth and on the sea, and all that is in them, singing: "To him who sits on the throne and to the Lamb be praise and honor and glory and power, for ever and ever!" - Revelation 5:11-13 (NIV)

THE RESURRECTION

> *"It means," said Aslan, "that though*
> *the Witch knew the Deep Magic,*
> *there is a magic deeper still which*
> *she did not know."*
>
> The Lion, The Witch and The Wardrobe

Aslan explains to the children that there is a deeper magic from before the dawn of time that the Witch did not know about. He explains that her knowledge only goes back to the dawn of time and—because of this—she is kept from understanding the deeper magic.

Aslan, who was there before the dawn of time, can read and understand the incantation fully. He knew that when a willing victim, who was innocent, was killed in the place of a traitor, "the Table would crack and Death itself would start working backwards."

This concept that the archenemy of God did not know the fullness of things or "the whole deal" is one that was shared by Rufinus of Aquileia, a theologian and historian (344-410 C.E.). He believed that Satan did not understand the true meaning and work of the cross until it occurred and he was defeated.

He wrote, "The purpose of the Incarnation… was that the divine virtue of the Son of God might be as it were a hook hidden beneath the form of human flesh… to lure on the prince of this age to a contest; that the Son might offer him his flesh as a bait and that then the divinity which lay beneath might catch him and hold him fast with its hook…. Then, as a fish when it seizes a baited hook not only fails to drag off the bait but is itself dragged out of the water to serve as food for others; so he that had the power of death seized the body of Jesus in death, unaware of the hook of divinity concealed therein. Having swallowed it, he was caught straightway;

the bars of hell were burst, and he was, as it were, drawn from the pit, to become food for others...."[14]

The main concept here is that the evil one is drawn in like a fish to a hook. Just as the Witch believed she had won the battle and would rule Narnia forever, Satan must have thought that he had defeated Jesus, the Son of God.

Jesus, who was with God from the beginning, entered into our world and took a body like ours so he could free us from the powers of sin and death. Because he is the Son of God he is fully divine, and because he is a man he is fully human. This reality allows him to perform the ultimate sacrifice of freeing mankind from the corruption of death and the consequences of sin. Because Jesus takes on a human body, which is capable of death, he can die for us all and pay the penalty for all of our sins. Because he is fully divine he has the ability to conquer death through the resurrection, breaking the curse of sin upon us.

Satan was not aware of this and thought that by achieving the death of Jesus on a cross he would win the world to himself. What a rude awakening it was for him when Jesus appeared in his full glory and triumphantly achieved the ultimate victory.

When Aslan, likewise, appears on the battlefield after having been resurrected, we are told that the Witch has "an expression of terror and amazement." Never in her wildest dreams did she expect Aslan to defeat death and to be victorious. Her curse and her influence in Narnia is over as Aslan lounges at her and takes her life.

We even see the animals and creatures that she made stone statues with her magical scepter coming back to life as Aslan breathes on them. Aslan's presence and majestic stature are emphatically made known as he roars, restores the statues to life, and defeats the evil White Witch.

When God created man he breathed on him and that breath is what made man become a living being. Jesus also breathed on his disciples after his resurrection, thus empowering them to do his work and imparting eternal life (Genesis 2:7; John 20:21-23). It is clear that there is power in the breath of God to impart life.

It is also arresting that in the Gospel of Matthew we are told that when Jesus died on the cross "…the earth shook and the rocks split. The tombs broke open and the bodies of many holy people who had died were raised to life" (Matthew 27:51-52, NIV).

This demonstrates the magnitude of what had occurred. We are told that the centurion and those guarding Jesus were "…terrified, and exclaimed, 'Surely he was the Son of God!'" (Matthew 27:54, NIV).

> *You hear a blast to end all blasts from a trumpet, and in the time that you look up and blink your eyes—it's over. On signal from that trumpet from heaven, the dead will be up and out of their graves, beyond the reach of death, never to die again. At the same moment and in the same way, we'll all be changed. In the resurrection scheme of things, this has to happen: everything perishable taken off the shelves and replaced by the imperishable, this mortal replaced by the immortal. Then the saying will come true:*
> > *Death swallowed by triumphant Life!*
> > *Who got the last word, oh, Death?*
> > *Oh, Death, who's afraid of you now?*
>
> *It was sin that made death so frightening and law-code guilt that gave sin its leverage, its destructive power. But now in a single victorious stroke of Life, all three—sin, guilt, death—are gone, the gift of our Master, Jesus Christ. Thank God! - 1 Corinthians 15:52-57 (MSG)*

THE GREAT KING

"He's wild you know. Not like a tame lion."

The Lion, The Witch and The Wardrobe

Like the roaring waves of the ocean, God's future actions are unpredictable and uncontrolled by anyone. When Aslan is described as wild and "not like a tame lion" we are reminded of the supreme ascendancy of God.

The movie *The Perfect Storm*'s plot is about a crew of fishermen in a swordfishing boat named Andrea Gail. They set out to the North Atlantic for a major catch and instead find a convergence of three storm fronts and a hurricane, which creates the "perfect storm."

In the film, which is based on a true story, monstrous waves are seen crashing down with great force while the fishing boat is tossed and displaced ferociously amid the rolling waves. As I watched the turbulent waves of the ocean moving with such great potency and power, I was reminded of the incredible strength and awesome sovereignty of God.

God can do whatever he wants, and the power he has is incomprehensible.

In the Disney film of *The Lion, The Witch and The Wardrobe* we see that even the Witch is barely able to stand in Aslan's presence. No one has any power over him—just like no one has any power over God. He is the creator and is sovereign over all.

In scripture Christ is described in this way: "He is the image of the invisible God, the firstborn over all creation. For by him all things were created: things in heaven and on earth, visible and invisible, whether thrones or powers or rulers or authorities; all things were created by him and for him. He is before all things, and in him all things hold together."

We are also told that God will "roar like a lion" and that "when he roars, his children will come trembling from the west" (Hosea 11:10, NIV), destroy the works of Satan (1 John 3:8), bring new life (John 10:10) and lay down his life for the sheep (John 10:11).

Aslan, for Narnia, symbolizes Christ—a savior and king who ushers in a new kingdom, brings eternal life, wipes away every tear, and who displays the qualities of both a great lion and a sacrificial lamb.

Aslan, like Christ, willingly sacrificed his life in a demonstration of love. Despite being a mighty lion whose thunderous roar causes all to tremble and stand in awe, we find that he is definitely motivated by love and that those who love him have nothing to fear. His big paws—which can lash out without a moment's notice at the enemy—handle those in his care with much tenderness and consideration.

> *He will cover you with feathers, and under his wings you will find refuge; his faithfulness will be your shield and rampart. - Psalm 91:4 (NIV)*

> *Oh, the depth of the riches of the wisdom and knowledge of God! How unsearchable his judgments, and his paths beyond tracing out! Who has known the mind of the Lord? Or who has been his counselor? - Romans 11:33-34 (NIV)*

MANY NAMES AND TITLES

"Aslan?" Said Mr. Beaver. "Why, don't you know? He's the King."

The Lion, The Witch and The Wardrobe

Aslan has many names and titles by which he is known. He is the King, the Creator of Narnia, Son of the Great Emperor-beyond-the-sea, the King of Beasts, and the Great Lion, who also comes to be known as a savior.

With many names and titles comes much responsibility. Aslan is given these names and titles because he inevitably is all of these things. It makes sense that God would have many names and titles as well. This is exactly what we find to be true in Christ.

In the book of Isaiah we find many names for Jesus. Isaiah 9:6, which presents a prophecy that has been fulfilled in Christ, reads, "For to us a child is born, to us a son is given, and the government will be on his shoulders. And he will be called Wonderful Counselor, Mighty God, Everlasting Father, Prince of Peace."

We discover that Jesus also is referred to as the King of Kings, Lord of Lords, Alpha and the Omega, Author of Life, the Chief Shepherd, Lamb of God, Son of God, Lion of Judah, and the Savior. And these are just some of the names he is given in scripture.

Some people we may know also have many titles and names that they go by as well. When this occurs, the individual, though well recognized and honored, has a lot to live up to. For instance, Lance Armstrong is known as a bicyclist, a champion, an author, a survivor, an advocate, a good citizen, a good father, etc. He has accumulated many accolades and, through the years, many titles. Because of this, people expect him to do and to be all of these things.

Yet Armstrong and all of his accomplishments and awards are nothing when compared to who God is and all that he has done. Nothing and no one can compare with the preeminence of God. How fortunate we are to have a God that has over 100 names—that he can live up to and uphold—that exemplify his greatness to all.

> *Help us, O God our Savior, for the glory of your name;*
> *deliver us and forgive our sins for your name's sake.*
> *- Psalm 79:9 (NIV)*

> *O LORD, our Lord, how majestic is your name in all*
> *the earth! You have set your glory above the heavens.*
> *From the lips of children and infants you have ordained*
> *praise because of your enemies, to silence the foe and*
> *the avenger. When I consider your heavens, the work of*
> *your fingers, the moon and the stars, which you have*
> *set in place, what is man that you are mindful of him,*
> *the son of man that you care for him? - Psalm 8:1-4*
> *(NIV)*

THE CONTRIBUTION

*Her hands trembled so much that she
could hardly undo the stopper, but
she managed it in the end and poured
a few drops into her brother's mouth.*

The Lion, The Witch and The Wardrobe

OUR PART TO PLAY

In this great story by C. S. Lewis we find that all the children and many others have a specific part to play in fulfilling the great plan of Aslan and the Emperor-beyond-the-Sea.

We see Peter assume the role of a leader of the army and lead the fight against the Witch. Peter held the fort while Aslan was gone and was even battling the Witch herself in a sword fight before the great Lion reappeared.

Edmund, who was badly wounded, played a significant part in the battle when he smashed down his sword on the Witch's wand and broke it. Before this, the Witch had been turning everyone that came close to her to stone, and it was appearing as if the battle was all but lost. Edmund's heroics gave Peter's army a chance and the extra time that was needed.

Lucy found herself in a situation where she could heal her brother Edmund with her special cordial. He was at the point of death, and with a few drops from Lucy's tonic he was revived. Lucy then helped many more who were wounded in the battlefield.

Susan protects and watches over her sister Lucy, the Beavers guide the children and help them find Aslan, and Mr. Tumnus helps Lucy and helps her return to the Wardrobe. All of these individuals have an important role to play in the larger drama.

We also have an important role to play in God's great plan to redeem the world. We must remember that we are significant and are called to something more than just ordinary living. When we open our eyes to this truth, we can begin to step into situations that are filled with purpose and meaning. We begin to find our talents and gifts and play our part in our Creator's plan. By drawing near to him and seeking our purpose in him, our spiritual gifts will be revealed. Our mentors can also help us in this regard. Once we have this knowledge, we can be quite sure that the great Lion will work with us and appear when we most need him. Just as he appeared to guide the children on the battlefield when the Witch was about to claim victory, he will make himself known to us and guide us in our darkest hour and time of need. When we step out in faith and contribute our part we have nothing to fear.

> *There are different ways to serve the same Lord, and we can each do different things. Yet the same God works in all of us and helps us in everything we do. - 1 Corinthians 12:5-6 (CEV)*

> *I have told you these things, so that in me you may have peace. In this world you will have trouble. But take heart! I have overcome the world. - John 16:33 (NIV)*

WORK TO BE DONE

"Our day's work is not yet over,"
he said. "And if the Witch is to be
finally defeated before bedtime we
must find the battle at once."
The Lion, The Witch and The Wardrobe

After Aslan brings the statues back to life he calls a meeting and tells everyone that there is still more work to be done. The creatures respond with excitement and rally behind the great Lion. The inevitable victory comes soon after.

After Jesus' resurrection he appeared to his disciples over a forty-day period. On one occasion, he was asked if he was going to restore the kingdom of Israel. He responded by saying, "It is not for you to know the times or dates the Father has set by his own authority. But you will receive power when the Holy Spirit comes on you; and you will be my witnesses in Jerusalem, and in all Judea and Samaria, and to the ends of the earth" (Acts 1:7-8, NIV).

Aslan tells the creatures that they "must find the battle at once" in order for the Witch to be defeated by bedtime. Jesus is not as specific in stating when the battle will end and tells us that it is not for us to know the time or date. But he does tell us that there is work to be done and that it is not over yet.

He calls the disciples and all his future followers to be his witnesses to the world. A witness is someone who testifies to the truth, like a witness in a courtroom who swears to tell nothing but the truth. The difference for us is that we are not supposed to wait until we are called into a courtroom; rather we are sent out by Jesus to tell the world the message of hope that Christ died for their sins, resurrected on the third day, and opened the door to eternal life for all who believe into him.

For this reason Jesus himself calls us the "salt" and "the light of the world" (Matthew 5:13-14, NIV). We are the Christ-bearers who bring the good news to the world. And we do not do it alone. Jesus promises to send us his Holy Spirit which brings power to help us complete this task.

When Aslan leads the creatures and Daughters of Eve into the battlefield to help Peter's waning army the victory comes soon after. We, too, can be led by God's Holy Spirit as we head onto the battlefield at work, school, church, or a ballgame. We are never alone, and the great Lion of Judah is always there to help us to complete the mission of reaching the world with the message of our Savior's sacrifice and tremendous love for us all. May we tap into the power that is available to us and fulfill our call to be Christ-bearers to a lost and needy world.

> *Then Jesus came to them and said, "All authority in heaven and on earth has been given to me. Therefore go and make disciples of all nations, baptizing them in the name of the Father and of the Son and of the Holy Spirit, and teaching them to obey everything I have commanded you. And surely I am with you always, to the very end of the age." - Matthew 28:18-20 (NIV)*

THE RESCUE

*Aslan! Aslan! I've found Mr. Tumnus.
Oh, do come quick."*

The Lion, The Witch and The Wardrobe

Lucy's first encounter in the land of Narnia is with the little Faun Tumnus, who invites her over for some tea and confesses his plan to kidnap her. He, of course, changes his mind and decides to help her get away. When she learns that he is in prison for having done this, she rallies all her brothers and sisters to look for him. Mr. Tumnus is the reason the children didn't initially turn back and return home—because he had helped Lucy the crew felt compelled to rescue him.

What an incredible joy Lucy must have felt when she was able to rescue and reunite with her special friend. We are told that after Mr. Tumnus is brought back to life, Lucy and the Faun begin holding hands and dancing for joy in celebration.

As we partner with God in the battle for our world, we must never lose focus of the purpose and the end for which we fight. Just like Peter, Susan, Lucy, and Edmund are caught up in a battle, so are we in the midst of a battle with spiritual ramifications. Satan wants to enslave and deceive the world into following his ways and he has brought a curse on mankind that leads to spiritual death.

Once we realize the gravity of all this and come to know the truth that Jesus' sacrifice sets us free from the curse of the law and death, we naturally become enthusiastic to share that good news with others. We understand that so many people are lost and headed in the wrong direction.

This reality stirs our soul and spirit into action. We yearn to bring people new hope and new life. The good news is that we can. And we do not need a magic wand or a special potion to accomplish

≈ 70 ≈

this. All we have to do is tell them the story of Jesus and allow them to decide if they want to believe into him or not.

Yet many of us hesitate to do this and miss out on experiencing the joy that Lucy felt when she found Mr. Tumnus. If we find ourselves hesitating to share our faith it is usually a result of fear, lack of knowledge, discomfort and/or laziness. All of these can be worked on and are not good excuses. It is also beneficial to go back and remind ourselves of what the Lion of Judah has done for us, tell ourselves that we are not alone, and meditate on what Jesus did for us on the cross.

If we do this, we will surely be ready to speak the message of Christ when the opportunity arises and experience the incredible joy of leading others to the fountain of life.

> How, then, can they call on the one they have not believed in? And how can they believe in the one of whom they have not heard? And how can they hear without someone preaching to them? And how can they preach unless they are sent? As it is written, "How beautiful are the feet of those who bring good news!"
> - Romans 10:14-15 (NIV)

> "... Christ changed us from enemies into his friends and gave us the task of making others his friends also."
> - 2 Corinthians 5:18 (GNB)

KINGS AND QUEENS

*Aslan solemnly crowned them and led
them to the four thrones...*
The Lion, The Witch and The Wardrobe

It is fitting that at the end of this great story that there is a happy
ending. For Narnia there is only good news as the prophecy is
fulfilled, the evil White Witch is defeated, the curse of the endless
winter is gone, and a new kingdom is established replacing the
tyranny of Jadis, the Witch.

The children who wandered into Narnia are now sitting on the four
glorious thrones of Cair Paravel. It is their destiny and calling to
serve in these roles.

As Christ-followers we are also told that someday we will reign with
Christ and will even judge angels (1 Corinthians 6:2-3). This is our
destiny and what awaits us. When we read the book of Revelations
we find that God will create a new earth and establish a new reign
(Revelations 21). We discover that in the end we win and are on the
winning side. Because of what Christ has done on the cross we can
now share in his inheritance.

May we honor the King and act in a worthy manner in this life so
that when we meet him in the next he can say, "Well done, good
and faithful servant." (Matthew 25:21, NIV)

Colossians chapter three tells us that we have died to our old
lives and that our lives are "now hidden with Christ in God"
(Colossians 3:3, NIV). It then instructs on how to continually
put to death what belongs to "our earthly nature" and how to put
on godly qualities that reflect Christ. I encourage you to read this
chapter and meditate on it. After doing this, pray that God will
work through you and help you surrender yourself to his plan
for your life. You may also want to read the scripture below while

substituting the words "you" or "your" with "I," "me," or "my" to personalize this prayer of the Apostle Paul and make it your own.

We do not have to wait until the end to become like Christ; we can begin the process today and reflect and represent the majestic heritage that we now have been given.

> *I pray also that the eyes of your heart may be enlightened in order that you may know the hope to which he has called you, the riches of his glorious inheritance in the saints, and his incomparably great power for us who believe. That power is like the working of his mighty strength.... - Ephesians 1:17 (NIV)*

A NEW WISDOM

And they made good laws and kept
the peace and saved good trees from
being unnecessarily cut down, and
liberated young dwarfs and young
satyrs from being sent to school, and
generally stopped busybodies and
interferers and encouraged ordinary
people who wanted to live and let
live.

The Lion, The Witch and The Wardrobe

The Pevensie children, who now sit on the four thrones at Cair Paravel, have become wise and mature in a short time. We are told that they made good laws, kept the peace and ruled justly.

These are the same children who days before were playing hide and go seek and who were staying with an old Professor in his home in the countryside because of the threat of the dangerous air raids of World War II.

What a transformation has occurred! But how? It is noteworthy to recall that the children were exposed to their purpose in life and to the great Aslan. These two factors led them to discover and embrace their roles.

The children were meant to partner with Aslan and help free Narnia from the curse of the White Witch—it was prophesied. When they realize this, their lives take on a new meaning because they know they are needed and valuable to Aslan and many others.

With this knowledge comes responsibility and obligation. How could they turn back to their old lives knowing all of this? The curiosity of what could have been and the regret of not having the boldness to live out their calling would be too much to bear.

Aslan's counsel and interaction with them provides the training they need to fulfill their call to leadership—much like Jesus' spending close to three years training and bonding with his disciples before the crucifixion. He left them when they were ready to assume his ministry and commanded them to "go into all the world and preach the good news to all creation " (Mark 16:15, NIV).

By spending time and associating with Aslan the children begin to look at things from his perspective and understand what needs to be done. They begin to see things from a totally different point of view—Aslan's. The children have a new found awareness of things, and the way they look at the world is radically different than before.

We, too, will gain Christ's perspective if we spend time with him daily through meditation, the Word of God, prayer, worship, service, or communion.

The Apostle Paul appeared to grasp the importance of this and writes, "…I consider everything a loss compared to the surpassing greatness of knowing Christ Jesus my Lord, for whose sake I have lost all things…" (Philippians 3:8, NIV).

And C. S. Lewis writes of the result of spending time with God and trusting in Christianity, "I believe in Christianity as I believe that the sun has risen: not only because I see it, but because by it I see everything else."[15]

When we encounter the great Lion of Judah and spend time with him, we begin to see things totally differently and with clarity. We as Christians see things through the lenses of Christ, and things make more sense because we are aligned with the truth. The distorted thoughts that used to lead us in rabbit trails to pain and disappointment are exchanged for truth that leads us to freedom and reality. Life lived in the truth and aligned to reality produces a much healthier and purposeful existence.

Another thing that helps is spending time with others who are in God's family. God definitely speaks to us through godly people and helps us to grow through small groups. This was his model (he led the first small group) and the way he works to transform us into the people he wants us to be.

The book and the film, *The Lion, The Witch and The Wardrobe,* present a story that reminds us of the Great Story. It is a story that can bring us closer to our Creator and help us wake up and see *our* purpose in life. Like Peter, Edmund, Susan, and Lucy we can also embark on a journey that will radically change our lives. The door is open wide and the great Lion of Judah is waiting for us to step into the wardrobe and join him in his quest to redeem our land. The adventures that lie ahead can fill pages and pages of books. Ponder things well, young traveler and may the great Lion be with you.

> *Now this is eternal life: that they may know you, the only true God, and Jesus Christ, whom you have sent. - John 17:3 (NIV)*

> *Jesus answered, "I am the way and the truth and the life. No one comes to the Father except through me." - John 14:6 (NIV)*

> *So then, men ought to regard us servants of Christ and as those entrusted with the secret things of God. Now it is required that those who have been given a trust must prove faithful. - 1 Corinthians 4:1-2 (NIV)*

END NOTES

1. John Ortberg, *The Life You've Always Wanted*, Michigan, Zondervan, 2002.

2. Genesis 1:2-5 (GNB)

3. Zondervan, *The NIV Study Bible*, Michigan, 1995.

4. John Piper, *Desiring God*, Oregon, Multnomah Publishers Oregon, 1996.

5. Brennan Manning, *Abba's Child*, Colorado, NavPress Publishing Group, 1994.

6. *Ibid*.

7. Sue Davis, *American Political Thought*, New Jersey, Prentice-Hall, 1996.

8. Manning, *op. cit.*

9. Catherine Dee, *The Girls' Book of Success*, United States, Megan Tingley, 2003.

10. Tom Jordan, *Pre*, United States, St. Martin's Press, 1997.

11. Saint Augustine, *City of God*, New York, Image Books, Doubleday, 1958.

12. Steve Hindalong, *City on a Hill – Reflections On Our Spiritual Journeys*, Oregon, Harvest House Publishers, 2000.

13. Hindalong, *ibid*.

14. Rufinus of Aquileia, *Documents of the Christian Church*, (Second Edition), New York, Oxford University Press, 1963.

15. C. S. Lewis, *The Weight of Glory*, New York, Harper Collins, 1980.

REFLECTIONS OF NARNIA

Study Guide

Chapter One Study Guide

1. How has curiosity gotten you in trouble in the past? Give an example. How can you prevent curiosity from leading you into trouble? Give an example of how discernment (good judgment) can help you when you become curious.

2. Why do you think man and woman were created in the image of God? How can you reflect the image of God in your life?

3. Describe a time when you were led by faulty thinking or a distorted thought. How did you feel when you realized you were wrong? What can you do when you discover that you have distorted thoughts? How can you discover more of them? Read Psalm 51:6, 139:23-24, and Proverbs 4:23.

4. How is God transforming you and making you a new person? Are you willing to continue to die to yourself to become a new creation in Christ? What do you think God is calling you to give up in your life? Read Luke 9:23-26; Luke 14:28-33.

5. List some common reasons why people might be afraid to come to Jesus. What are some reasons that you have been afraid to come to Jesus in the past? What can you do when you are afraid to draw near to God?

6. Describe a situation where God answered your prayer(s). Give an example of how he has worked through you to help another person. Describe how this made you feel.

Chapter One - Thoughts and Notes

Chapter Two Study Guide

1. Have you ever had a hard time believing in something you could not explain? Why do you think this can be very difficult for many people? Give one example of a time where you did believe in something that you could not explain and you found it beneficial.

2. Have you experienced a relationship with the living God? If not, what do you think keeps you from experiencing this? If you have experienced a relationship with God, what do you think enabled you to do this?

3. Have you put on your "royal robes?" Read Colossians 3:10-12. In this verse it implies that we have the choice to put on a new wardrobe. Have you made this choice? Discuss (or write down) what can occur in your life if you put on Christ's new wardrobe.

4. How have you ignored God's calling on your life or doing what he has asked of you? If so, why do you think that you have done this?

5. What are some things that you are hanging on to in your life that are unhealthy? What keeps you from surrendering these things to Christ? Are you willing to trust God and let go? If so, consider finding someone who you can meet with regularly (accountability partner) to share this with and be accountable to.

Chapter Two - Thoughts and Notes

Chapter Three Study Guide

1. What are some tools (spiritual armor) that God has given you for the battle against Satan? How are you doing in regards to using these tools? What can you do to improve your use of these tools?

2. How have you fallen for the delicacies of the evil one in your past? Are you still stuck in a particular sin? What can you do to gain freedom and avoid falling into the traps of the devil?

3. In what ways have people in positions of authority, society, television, peers, family, culture, or trends influenced your thinking in a negative way? As you write down these things, on another column you may want to write down what scripture has to say about these things. If needed you can ask a friend to help you find scriptures that combat the negative ideas, views, or thoughts.

4. How have the negative messages of the world (society, peers, family, etc.) affected your Christian walk negatively?

5. Have you experienced God's forgiveness in your life? Why or why not? How can you help others experience God's forgiveness in their lives? Is there anyone that you need to forgive? If so, are you willing to let go of your resentment and forgive them? Why or why not?

6. Read Ephesians 3:17-19 and Romans 8:38-39 by replacing the word "you" with "I." After reading these verses in this way write a prayer to God thanking him for all that he has done for you.

Chapter Three - Thoughts and Notes

Chapter Four Study Guide

1. Are there times where you feel that you need to earn God's love in your life and you revert back to the Old Covenant way of thinking? How can the truth of us having total access to God revolutionize your life? Take some time to be real with God and share your deepest hurts and concerns.

2. What stands in your way of getting on your knees and worshipping God with all your heart?

3. Can you schedule a non-negotiable time daily where you can spend quality time with God?

4. How can reflecting on God's power and sovereignty help us to understand him better and our selves (in relation to him)?

5. How can reflecting on the many names of God help you to appreciate him in more in depth way? Practice meditating on some of the names of God this week in your quiet time. Try to also look up some new passages.

Chapter Four - Thoughts and Notes

Chapter Five Study Guide

1. What are some of your talents and abilities? How can you use them to serve God and partner with his plan to redeem the world?

2. Do you know what your spiritual gifts are? Why or Why not? Read 1 Corinthians Chapter 12 and share what you think may be your spiritual gifts with someone. Make a commitment this month to try to use some of the spiritual gifts that you have (or may have) to serve others. (By trying out different gifts you will eventually discover your spiritual gifts).

3. How can you be the "salt" and "light" of the world in a practical and real way? How can you be a witness for Christ?

4. What are some reasons that you have hesitated to share your faith in Christ in the past? How can you work on these reasons that have stood in your way of experiencing the joy of sharing your faith?

5. How have you begun to see things from a different perspective since you became a Christ follower? Describe how your worldview has changed? How have other believers helped you grow spiritually? How can you help others grow spiritually in their walk with Christ?

Chapter Five - Thoughts and Notes

THE AUTHOR

Eddie Zacapa was born in Santa Clara, California. He has worked with Campus Crusade for Christ for many years and was the founder of The Next Step Ministries. Eddie is a domestic violence counselor, and he is also the author of *Matrix Reflections*.

He earned a Bachelor of Science degree in Journalism from San Jose State University and a Bachelor of Science degree in Bible and Theology from William Jessup University. He currently attends and serves as a Small Group Director at Western Hills Church in San Mateo, California. Eddie and his wife, Rachel, live in Mountain View, California. They have two sons, Andrew and Adam, and two turtles.

CPSIA information can be obtained at www.ICGtesting.com
Printed in the USA
LVOW131618131112

307154LV00008B/115/A